dyework

dyework

Creative fabric decoration to enhance the home

Judith Gussin
Photography by Michelle Garrett

southwater

This edition is published by Southwater

Southwater is an imprint of
Anness Publishing Limited
Hermes House
88-89 Blackfriars Road
London SE1 8HA
tel. 020 7401 2077
fax 020 7633 9499

Distributed in the UK by
The Manning Partnership
251-253 London Road East
Batheaston
Bath BA1 7RL
tel. 01225 852 727
fax 01225 852 852

Distributed in the USA by
Anness Publishing Inc.
27 West 20th Street
Suite 504
New York NY 10011
tel. 212 807 6739
fax 212 807 6813

Distributed in Australia by
Sandstone Publishing
Unit 1, 360 Norton Street
Leichhardt
New South Wales 2040
tel. 02 9560 7888
fax 02 9560 7488

© 2000 Anness Publishing Limited

1 3 5 7 9 10 8 6 4 2

Publisher: Joanna Lorenz
Project Editor: Simona Hill
Photographer: Michelle Garrett
Designer: Lilian Lindblom
Editorial Reader: Diane Ashmore

CONTENTS

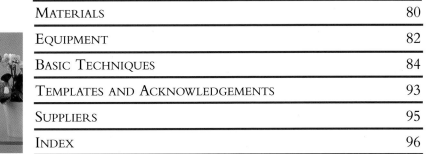

INTRODUCTION

Creative dyeing is a very exciting craft and opens up a wealth of possibilities for using hand-dyed fabrics and threads. Starting with a small range of cold-water reactive dyes and a limited amount of equipment – most of which you will already have – you can create an endless variety of multicoloured fabrics. If you also use acid dyes for wool and silk you can extend your options even further, and fabrics can be sprayed and painted with dye solutions, fabric paints and printing inks. Fabrics suitable for dyeing range from basic calico (muslin) and cotton poplin to luxurious silk satin and textured silks.

The techniques section describes in detail all the dyeing methods you will need for the projects, whether you are spraying a small amount of material to make lavender bags, dyeing a length of muslin in pastel colours to make a beaded curtain, or using a combination of reactive and acid dyes to dye fabrics and threads for a wallhanging inspired by Indian textiles.

Full instructions are included for dyeing and making up each project and a comprehensive basic technqiues section tells you all you need to know to get started. When the project is complete, you may like to embellish your pieces using machine or hand embroidery, beading and shisha glass. A full set of templates is included. Experiment with different fabrics, thread and dye techniques and solutions, then add your choice of decoration to make unique and individual hand-crafted items.

Deborah Barker

VELVET-EDGED THROW

If you have a store of warm, wool blankets you no longer use on the bed, colour one softly using dye to create a beautiful throw with a luxurious velvet ribbon trim.

YOU WILL NEED
thick wool fabric
scissors
hand dye
large dye bath
iron and pressing cloth
satin bias binding
sewing machine
matching sewing thread
pins
needle
ruffled ribbon
wide velvet ribbon

1 Trim the fabric to a square or rectangular shape and wash to remove any dressing. Make up the dye in a large container and check the colour on a sample piece (which you can take with you when choosing ribbons for the edging). After dyeing, rinse the fabric very thoroughly and press under a damp cloth when dry.

2 To bind the edges, machine-stitch satin bias binding to the right side all round the edge. Fold the binding over to the wrong side, and baste in place. Either machine or hand stitch in place on the wrong side to finish, folding in the excess neatly at the corners.

3 On the right side, stitch a length of ruffled ribbon close to the edge of the binding to cover it. Stitch along both sides of the ribbon using matching thread.

4 Cut four lengths of ribbon to fit the edges of the throw. Join the lengths by stitching diagonally across each corner, with right sides together, to create mitres.

5 Pin the ribbon carefully to the throw and stitch down on each side by hand or machine. Take care when pinning velvet as it can mark easily.

PARTY TABLECLOTH

The dramatic border of triangles around this cloth looks like a row of fluttering pennants.
Its colours and shapes are echoed in the multicoloured stitching on the cloth. Space-dye the fabric
using the reactive dye method for deep colours described in the techniques section.

YOU WILL NEED

for a 1.4m/55in square cloth, excluding border, 3.75m/4yd
cotton poplin 1.5m/59in wide
tape measure
scissors
cold-water reactive dyes in blue, reddish blue, black, yellow,
lemon yellow, red, violet and green
washing soda (sodium carbonate)
dyeing equipment including plastic trays and bags, glass jars,
measuring spoons and beakers
paper
tailor's chalk
long ruler
sewing machine
multicoloured machine embroidery thread
matching sewing threads
pins
tacking (basting) thread
needle

1 Cut the poplin into four lengths ready for dyeing: 2.25m/2½yd for the dark blue cloth, bindings and triangles; and three pieces 50cm/20in long for the contrast colours. Use stock solutions of 5ml/1tsp dye in 300ml/½ pint hot water throughout, and fix the colours by the hot water method.

DARK BLUE	YELLOW	DEEP PINK	GREEN
• 540ml/19fl oz blue dye solution + 180ml/6fl oz soda solution	• 75ml/2½fl oz yellow dye solution + 40ml/1½fl oz soda solution + 75ml/2½fl oz water	• 150ml/5fl oz red dye solution + 70ml/2¼fl oz soda solution	• 30ml/1fl oz yellow + 120ml/4fl oz green dye solutions + 75ml/2½fl oz soda solution
• 540ml/19fl oz reddish blue dye solution + 180ml/6fl oz soda solution	• 75ml/2½fl oz lemon yellow dye solution + 40ml/1½fl oz soda solution + 75ml/2½fl oz water	• 75ml/2½fl oz violet dye solution + 40 ml/1½fl oz soda solution	• 50ml/2fl oz yellow + 100ml/3½fl oz blue dye solutions + 75ml/2½floz soda solution
• 180ml/6fl oz black dye solution + 90ml/3fl oz soda solution			

2 Enlarge the triangle pattern at the back of the book to measure 20cm/8in long, plus 1cm/½in seam allowances. Cut 14 triangles (seven pairs) in each of the four colours, and four strips 5 x 1.5m/2 x 59in in blue to bind the edge of the tablecloth.

3 Using tailor's chalk, mark a diamond grid on the tablecloth, spacing the lines 20cm/8in apart. Draw the first line from diagonal corner to corner and work from the centre outwards.

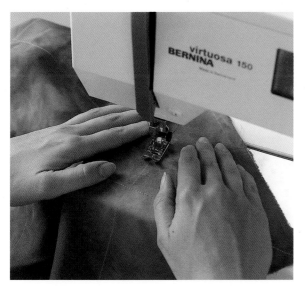

4 Machine stitch along the chalked lines using multicoloured machine embroidery thread and a straight stitch. Use coloured thread in the bobbin, in case the chalk lines prove difficult to remove.

5 Using matching thread, sew each pair of triangles together with a 1cm/½in seam allowance, along the two bias edges.

▶

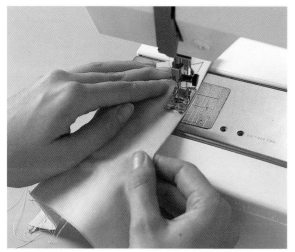

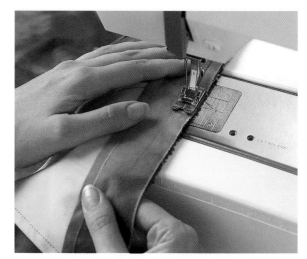

6 Trim the corners, turn through, pushing the point of the triangle out, and press. Top stitch close to each edge using multi-coloured machine embroidery thread. Tack (baste) together the unstitched edges of each triangle. There will be seven triangles in each colour.

7 With right sides together, pin and tack the raw edge of the triangles to the edge of the cloth, pointing inwards, lining them up with the machine-stitched grid. Maintain the colour sequence red, yellow, green, and blue. Press under one long edge of the bindings by 1cm/½in. On two opposite sides, with right sides together, pin and stitch the unpressed edge of the binding to the edge of the cloth.

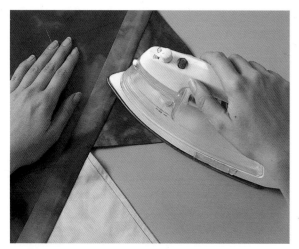

8 Press the binding to the wrong side and neatly slipstitch the turned-under edge in place, to cover the raw edges of the triangles. Repeat for the other two edges, turning the raw edges under neatly at the corners.

9 Top stitch the edge of the tablecloth using multicoloured thread. Use a non-biological detergent when laundering. The addition of a specialist non-ionic detergent will also help to stop any colours from running.

BEADED CURTAIN

For an ethereal, delicate summer window dressing, space-dye a length of muslin in a mix of pastel colours, then decorate it with a tracery of machine embroidery and tiny pearl beads.

YOU WILL NEED
curtain weight muslin to fit window,
allowing 15cm/6in per drop for hems
and casings, plus shrinkage
cold-water reactive dyes in red, blue,
lemon yellow and green
washing soda (sodium carbonate)
dyeing equipment including latex gloves,
measuring spoons, beakers, glass jars,
stirring rods and large plastic tray
iron and thick towel
sewing machine
multicoloured machine embroidery
thread (floss)
scissors
needle
pearl and/or glass beads
matching sewing thread

**RECIPE FOR 2.5M/2¾YD
(250G/9OZ) MUSLIN**

RED

• 19ml/4 tsp red dye solution + 40ml/
1½fl oz soda solution + water to make
250ml/9fl oz

BLUE

• 19ml/4 tsp blue dye solution +
40ml/1½fl oz soda solution + water to
make 250ml/9fl oz

GREEN

• 8ml/1½ tsp lemon yellow + 12ml/
2½ tsp green dye solutions + 40ml/
1½fl oz soda solution + water to make
250ml/9fl oz

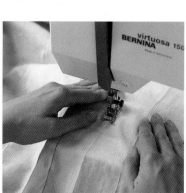

1 Wash and dry the muslin and space-dye using cold-water reactive dyes by the method for pale colours described in the techniques section. Use stock dye solutions of 2.5ml/½ tsp dye in 300ml/½ pint hot water. Wash the fabric and iron dry. Tidy the side edges. Fold in half lengthways. Working on a quarter of the curtain at a time, press lengthways folds 3–4cm/1¼–1½in apart.

2 Using complementary multi-coloured machine embroidery thread (floss), stitch along the pressed lines. Begin varying distances from the top, and stitch to the bottom of the curtain. Start each row with a few reverse stitches. Cut the bobbin thread at the top but leave the front thread hanging. Repeat across the curtain, then press.

3 Stitch a 5cm/2in double hem at the foot and a 2.5cm/1in casing at the top. Thread a fine needle with the loose thread at the top of each row and attach a fine pearl or glass bead. Add further beads at random intervals down the rows. Press lightly on the wrong side, resting the curtain on a thick towel. Ensure the heat of the iron is not high enough to melt the beads.

RAINBOW COSMETIC BAG

Painting dyes on to sheer fabric gives a soft, pretty effect, even when the colours are vibrant.
This little bag is lined with shower curtain fabric to make it water-resistant.

YOU WILL NEED
0.5m/½yd cotton lawn or poplin
cold-water reactive dyes in red, yellow and blue
urea and washing soda (sodium carbonate)
dyeing equipment including latex gloves, measuring spoons,
beakers and stirring rods
paintbrush
plastic sheet, plastic piping, plastic bag and clothes pegs (pins)
2m/2yd No 6 cotton piping cord
plastic box
tape measure
scissors
0.5m/½yd shower curtain fabric
sewing machine
matching sewing thread
pins
tacking (basting) thread
needle
large safety pin

1 Colour the cotton lawn or poplin and piping cord using the painting with reactive dyes technique. Put the cord in a small plastic box for 48 hours. Wash the fabric and iron dry. Cut one piece 75 x 27cm/30 x 11in, and a piece of shower curtain 55 x 27cm/22 x 11in. Fold the lining in half and stitch the side seams with a 1cm/½in seam allowance. Fold the dyed fabric in half and stitch both side seams down 15cm/6in from the top; leave a 2cm/¾in gap, then stitch to the bottom. Press the side seams open.

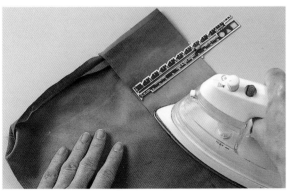

2 Press under 0.5cm/¼in around the top edge of the bag and then turn down and press a 9cm/3½in hem. Turn the bag right side out.

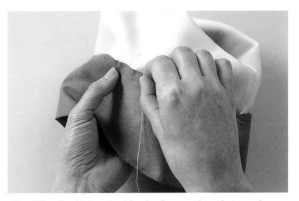

3 Slip the lining inside the bag and tuck it under the hem. Pin the bottom of the hem, then turn the bag inside out and tack (baste) close to the edge. ▶

4 Turn the bag right side out. With a co-ordinating thread in the needle and bobbin, machine stitch along the tacking line.

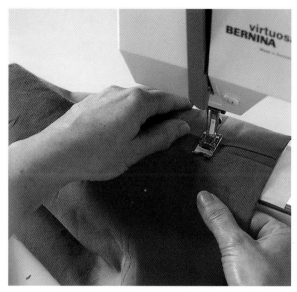

5 To make the casing for the piping, add two more rows of stitching, 7cm/2¾in and 5cm/2in from the top, to correspond with the side seam gaps.

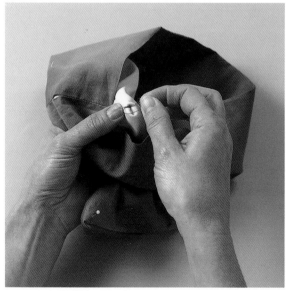

6 Turn the bag inside out and catch the lining to the bag at the lower corners with one or two stitches. Turn the bag right side out and press lightly, ensuring the heat of the iron does not melt the shower curtain fabric.

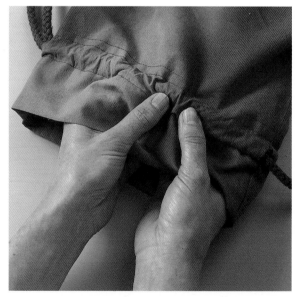

7 Cut two lengths of piping cord each 80cm/32in. Attach a safety pin to one end and thread through a side opening, around the casing, and return to the same opening. Repeat with the second cord through the other opening. Knot the cord ends.

LAVENDER BAGS

Pyramid-shaped lavender bags have been spray-dyed and decorated with beads. They are made using a loosely woven fabric, which allows the scent of the lavender through.

YOU WILL NEED

scraps of white cotton fabric such as stiff cheesecloth (muslin) or heat-printed voile
reactive dye solutions in red, blue and violet, made up in chemical water (see basic techniques)
spray-dyeing equipment, including latex gloves, spray bottles, measuring beakers and syringes
paper
pencil
scissors
sewing machine
matching sewing thread
narrow ribbon
dried lavender
teaspoon
needle
pearl beads

1 Wash and dry, then spray-dye the fabric using the method described in the techniques section. Enlarge the template at the back of the book and cut out, carefully marking the positions *a*, *b*, *c*, *d*, *e* and *f*. Use the template to cut out the fabric for the bags, matching the direction of the grain. One triangle makes one bag.

Above: Delicate pearl beads complement the muted colours of these lavender bags.

2 Using 0.5cm/¼in seam allowances throughout, fold point *a* to point *b* and stitch down to *d*. ▶

19

3 Fold point *c* to meet point *ab* and stitch down to *e* using a 0.5cm/¼in seam allowance. The fabric should resemble a pyramid shape.

4 Fold a 10cm/4in length of ribbon into a loop. Pin the ends to align with the raw edges of the fabric at point *abc*, at the top of the pyramid. Pin and stitch down to point *f*. Turn right side out.

5 Fill the sachet loosely with lavender and neatly slipstitch the opening closed.

6 Decorate with small pearl beads. Stitch the beads around the base of the pyramid, securing the thread every three or four beads with a back stitch.

TIE-DYE DUVET COVER

The single clear blue used for this design combined with the bold square scheme makes a simple, contemporary bedcover.

YOU WILL NEED
white cotton and linen fabrics with
contrasting textures
iron
coins, marbles and beads
rubber bands and strong thread
machine dye and salt (or hand dye and dye bath)
set (t-) square
scissors
needle
tacking (basting) thread
white duvet cover
fabric marker or tailor's chalk
pins
piece of cardboard
sewing machine
matching sewing thread

1 Wash the white fabrics to remove any dressing and iron flat while still damp. Tie circular items of different sizes, such as coins, marbles or beads, into half the fabric pieces, securing them tightly using rubber bands.

2 To create the stripe effect, pleat the remaining fabric accordion-fashion, keeping the pleats about 3cm/1¼in wide. Tie the pleats using strong thread or string. Space the ties evenly on each piece of fabric, but vary the spacing between pieces of cloth, to give stripes of different proportions.

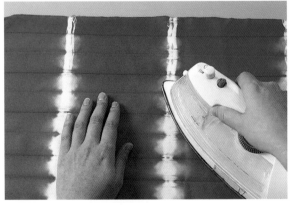

3 Dye the tied bundles using machine dye and following the manufacturer's instructions. (If your washing machine is not suitable, use hand dye in a dye bath.) Remove the bindings and wash away all excess dye. Iron the fabric flat while still damp.

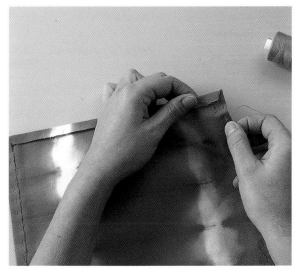

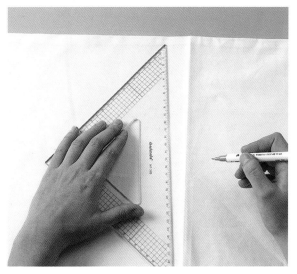

4 Cut the dyed fabrics into 27cm/11in squares (this includes 1cm/½in seam allowances on all sides.) Turn in the seam allowance and tack (baste), folding the corners in neatly. Press each square.

5 Iron a crease down the centre of the duvet cover. Measure and mark 25cm/10in down the central crease from the top seam, using a set (t-) square and fabric marker.

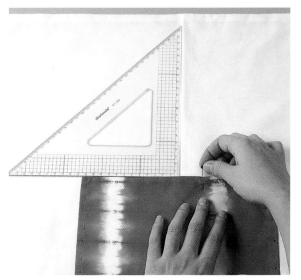

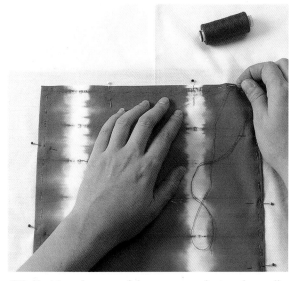

6 Centre the first square on the crease, with the top edge on the 25cm/10in mark. Pin in position making sure it is square with the top seam.

7 Position the rest of the top row, placing them all one square's width from each other horizontally, and one square's height from the top. Tack the squares firmly into place (insert a piece of cardboard into the cover so that you don't accidentally sew through both sides). ▶

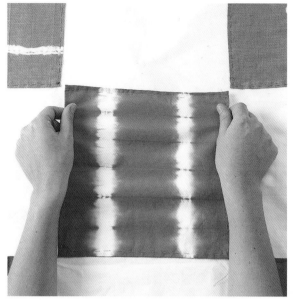

8 Pin and tack (baste) the remaining fabric squares, making sure that they are all square to each other and the sides of the cover.

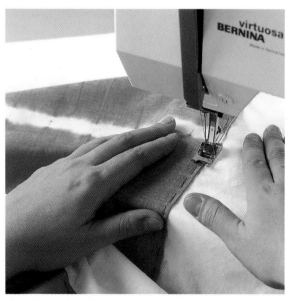

9 Using thread to match the dye colour, machine-stitch round each square close to the edge. Remove all tacking stitches. Wash the cover according to the dye manufacturer's guidelines.

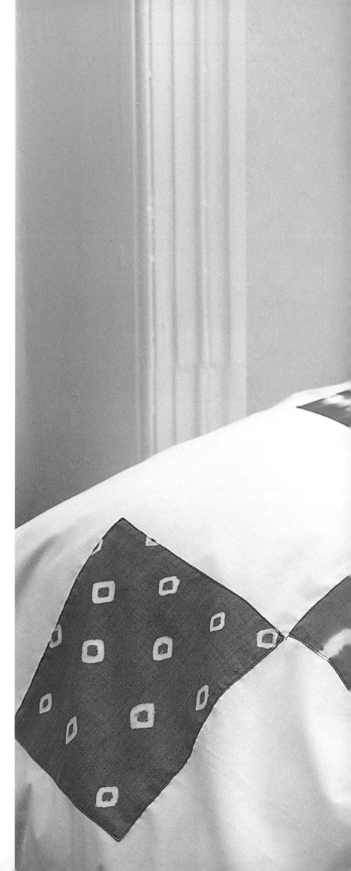

BLOCK-PRINTED CUSHION

Printing with fabric dyes presents another creative method of dyeing fabric using colours and intensity in an exciting way. Experiment with a variety of stamps and printing blocks.

YOU WILL NEED
ready-made cotton-covered chair pad
extra cotton or calico for experimenting
cold-water reactive dyes in green and yellow
washing soda (sodium carbonate)
dyeing equipment, including latex gloves, plastic bowl,
measuring spoons, beakers and stirring rods
cardboard
felt-tipped pen
newspaper
scissors
pencil
ruler
polystyrene (styrofoam) tray
piece of wool blanket
plastic spoon
fabric printing inks in yellow, green and blue
small offcut (scrap) of 1.75cm/¾in wood
fine paintbrush
iron

RECIPE FOR 100G/3½OZ FABRIC

• 25ml/5 tsp green dye solution+ 25ml/5 tsp yellow dye solution

+ 25ml/5 tsp soda solution + water to make 350ml/12fl oz

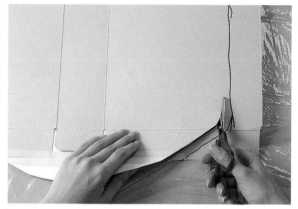

1 Remove the pad from the cushion cover. Wash and dry the cover, then dye using the cold water reactive dye method for pale colours, adding an extra piece of fabric for experimenting. Use stock solutions of 2.5ml/½ tsp dye in 300ml/½ pint hot water. Cut a piece of cardboard to fit snugly inside the cover.

2 Draw around the cardboard on a folded newspaper and cut this out about 0.5cm/¼in smaller than the cardboard. Cut about two newspapers for each side of the cushion, and slide half the sheets into the cover on top of the cardboard to make a pad.

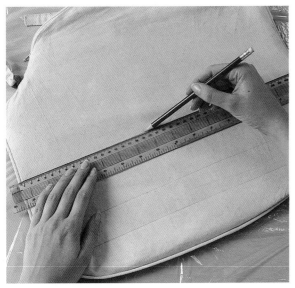

3   With a pencil and ruler draw very light horizontal lines across the cushion as a guide for printing. Space the lines a ruler's width apart.

4   Make a printing pad by lining a polystyrene (styrofoam) tray with a piece of blanket and, with a plastic spoon, put small amounts of yellow, green and blue fabric printing inks on to the pad.

5   Practise printing first on a spare piece of fabric. Dip the block of wood into each of the inks, trying to combine the colours on the block, and then press down firmly on the fabric. You may get a second print from the block before reloading with ink.

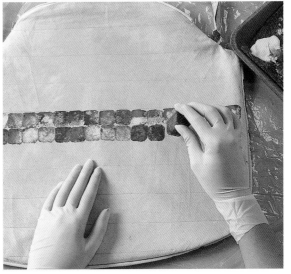

6   Print the cushion pad starting from the middle, working downwards in horizontal lines. Use the pencil guidelines to keep the printed rows straight.

7 When the first section is complete, turn the cover around to print the rest. The picture shows the effects of using different printing blocks.

8 Retouch the edges and any piping using a fine paintbrush. Print on one side of the cushion ties. Allow to dry for 48 hours.

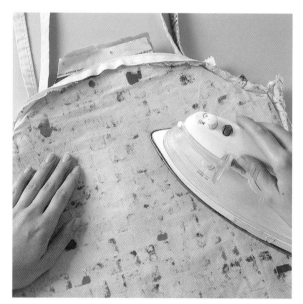

9 Remove the cardboard and newspaper and turn inside out. Reinsert the cardboard. Press the reverse side of the printing, following the manufacturer's instructions to fix (set) the inks. Remove the cardboard and turn right side out.

10 Turn the seat cover over, reinsert the cardboard and add the unused shaped newspaper. Mark with a pencil and print, then leave to dry. Finish by printing the other side of the ties, allow to dry and fix as before.

SPACE-DYED TEDDY BEAR RUG

This colourful rug for a child's room is made from space-dyed felt, which makes a rich background for appliquéd felt teddy bears. Start with a large square of felt, as it will shrink by as much as 30% during dyeing and drying. The finished rug is 90cm/36in in diameter.

YOU WILL NEED

white wool/viscose felt 1.4m/55in square for the rug, and 50 x 100cm/19½ x40in for the teddy bears
cold-water reactive dyes in red, blue, yellow and lemon yellow
washing soda (sodium carbonate)
dyeing equipment, including latex gloves, large plastic tray, measuring beakers, glass jars and stirring rods
iron
1m/1yd calico 1.5m/59in wide
3m/3¼yd white cotton or viscose fringe or braid
paper
tape measure
string
pencil
scissors
heavyweight iron-on interfacing
pins
thin cardboard
glue stick
craft knife
cutting mat
stranded embroidery thread (floss)
needle
matching sewing thread
fusible bonding web
fabric marker
ruler
sewing machine

1 Dye the felt for the rug and the teddy bears using the cold water reactive space-dyed method for deep colours (see techniques). Use stock solutions of 2.5ml/½ tsp dye in 300ml/½ pint hot water. After dyeing and washing, the wool/viscose felt can be dried in a tumble drier.

2 Space-dye the calico for the backing and bias binding using the cold water method for deep colours as before. Wash and iron dry the fabric. Space-dye a fringe or braid using the same recipe: weigh the dry fringe and adjust the amount of dye needed. Reshape the fringe while damp.

RECIPE FOR 1.4M/55IN SQUARE FELT FOR THE RUG (320G/11½OZ)
- 210ml/7½fl oz red dye solution + 100ml/3½fl oz soda solution + water to make 350ml/12fl oz
- 185 ml/6½fl oz blue dye solution + 90ml/3fl oz soda solution + water to make 350ml/12fl oz
- 160ml/5½fl oz yellow dye solution + 90ml/3fl oz soda solution + water to make 350ml/12fl oz

RECIPE FOR 50 x 100CM/20 x 40IN FOR THE TEDS (70G/2¼OZ)
- 100ml/3½fl oz yellow dye solution + 40ml/1½fl oz soda solution
- 100ml/3½fl oz lemon yellow dye solution + 40ml/1½fl oz soda solution

RECIPE FOR 1M/40IN OF 1.5M/59IN-WIDE CALICO (240G/8½OZ)
- 160ml/5½fl oz red dye solution + 75ml/2½fl oz soda solution + water to make 260 ml/9½fl oz
- 140ml/4½fl oz blue dye solution + 70ml/2¼fl oz soda solution + water to make 260ml/9½fl oz
- 120ml/4fl oz yellow dye solution + 60ml/2fl oz soda solution + water to make 260ml/9½fl oz

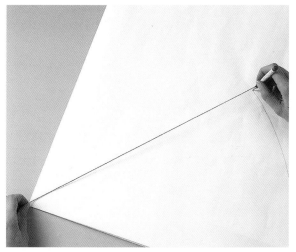

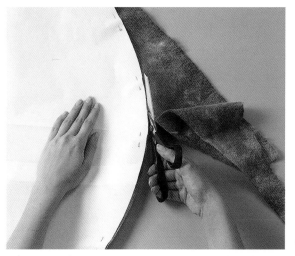

3 To make a pattern for the rug fold a 90cm/35½in square of thin paper into four quarters. Hold the end of a 45cm/17¾in length of string in the folded corner, attach the other end to a pencil and draw a quarter of a circle. Cut along this curve and then open out the pattern.

4 Using the paper pattern, cut out a circle of iron-on interfacing. Pin the interfacing web side down to the wrong side of the felt. Iron the interfacing to the felt starting from the centre and working outwards. Cut out carefully. Use a damp cloth for pressing if necessary.

5 Copy the teddy bear design from the back of the book and enlarge on a photocopier to a height of 14cm/5½in. Stick the copy on to thin cardboard. Cut out using a craft knife and cutting mat. Use the template to cut out eight teddy bears from yellow felt. Embroider the features using stranded thread (floss).

6 Pin the bears in position in a circle, 10cm/4in from the edge of the rug. Make sure each bear is evenly spaced from the next. Neatly slipstitch each bear to the rug using a co-ordinating sewing thread. Iron the back of the rug.

7 Using the pattern, cut out a circle from the dyed calico backing. Iron fusible bonding web to the wrong side, cutting and piecing the web to fit accurately. Use a hot iron protected by a cloth. Remove the paper backing. Place the rug right side down on a flat surface with the calico on top. Fuse the backing in place, ironing from the centre outward. Trim the edges. ▶

8 With a piece of calico 25 x 90cm/10 x 35½in, make 3m/3¼yd bias binding to go around the rug. Fold the fabric corner diagonally down to find the true bias. Mark lines 4cm/ 1½in apart, parallel with the fold. Make a diagonal fold up on the last line and cut off both folded corners to make a rhombus.

9 With right sides together, join the ends of the strips, with one strip width extending beyond the edge at each side. Cut along the marked line at one end and continue in a circular movement.

10 Press under a 0.5cm/¼in seam down one long side and one short end of the binding. With right sides together and raw edges aligned, pin the binding around the rug. Stitch, with a 1cm/½in seam allowance. Overlap the ends by 1cm/½in.

11 Press the binding outwards then fold it over the edge of the rug, and slipstitch the folded edge in place on the back. Press flat. On the front, slipstitch the fringe in place over the binding, overlapping the join (seam) neatly.

SPACE-DYED FELT TEDDY BEARS

These dear little bears are made from space-dyed felt. You need a piece about 20 x 30cm/ 8 x 12in for each bear, so you can use scraps left over from larger projects or scale down the dyeing recipes and dye as much felt as you need, remembering to allow for 30% shrinkage.

YOU WILL NEED

thin cardboard

glue stick

scissors

lightweight iron-on interfacing

space-dyed felt in two contrasting colours

pencil

stranded embroidery thread (floss)

needle

pins

matching sewing thread

polyester toy filling (stuffing)

1 Enlarge the teddy bear template to 14cm/5½in high. Stick the copy on to a piece of thin cardboard and cut it out. Iron lightweight interfacing to the wrong side of the felt. Using the template, draw two bears on the interfacing. Cut out with sharp scissors. Cut out two tiny ovals from contrasting felt for the paws and two slightly larger ones for the feet.

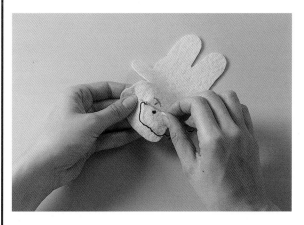

2 Using stranded embroidery thread (floss), stitch the eyes in satin stitch and the mouth in straight stitch. Stitch on the paws.

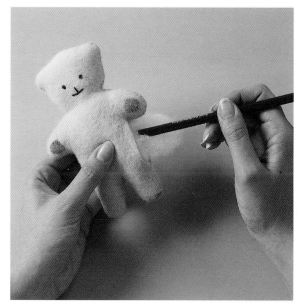

3 Pin the front to the back, wrong sides together, and stitch with small oversewing stitches using matching sewing thread. Leave an opening under one arm for stuffing.

4 Firmly stuff the bear carefully using small pieces of toy filling (stuffing) and pushing it into the feet and paws using the end of a pencil. Neatly slipstitch the opening shut.

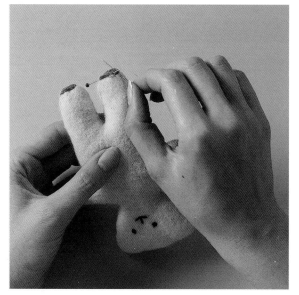

5 Sew the remaining felt shapes to the feet over the seam lines. Tie a matching thread firmly around the bear's neck to give him a chin.

Above: This teddy bear is an ideal project for a child to sew.

BATIK NAPKIN

Batik is a resist technique in which wax is applied to protect areas of the fabric so that they do not absorb dye. For these napkins, the hardened wax is cracked so that dye seeps into the crevices to produce a stylish tracery of fine lines.

YOU WILL NEED
white square lightweight linen napkins
yellow machine dye, or hand dye and a dye bath
salt
latex gloves
iron
ruler
fabric marker
fabric painting frame
fine-pointed flat-headed pins
batik wax
wax pot or double boiler
portable electric or gas ring (burner)
kitchen thermometer
medium artist's paintbrush
spare piece of fabric
shallow dye bath large enough for napkins to lie flat
spoon
dark indigo-blue hand dye
lining paper

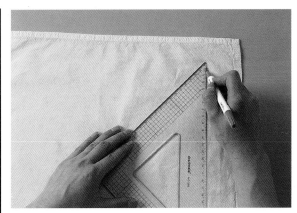

1 Dye the napkins yellow using a machine dye. (Use hand dye if your machine is not suitable.) Wash the napkins to remove any excess dye and iron flat while still damp. Draw a border around each napkin 5cm/2in from the edges with a fabric marker.

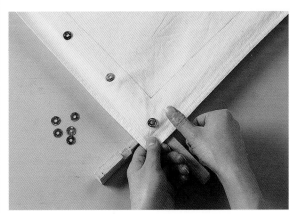

2 Stretch the napkin on a fabric painting frame using fine-pointed flat-headed pins. Heat some batik wax in a wax pot or double boiler to a steady 80°C/176°F using a small gas or electric ring (burner) that can be kept hot where you are working. ▶

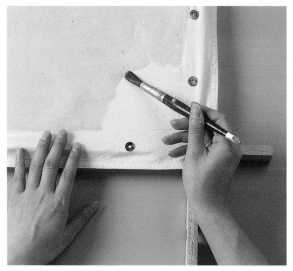

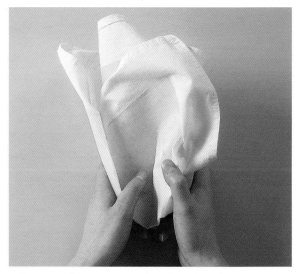

3 Using a medium artist's paintbrush, fill in the centre square of the napkin with wax. The wax should leave the fabric semi-transparent: if it remains opaque the wax is not hot enough (always test it on a spare piece of cloth before starting the final piece).

4 Leave the wax to cool and harden, then remove the napkin from the frame and crumple it in your hands, cracking the surface. The more cracks that are made, the more the dye will penetrate the fabric.

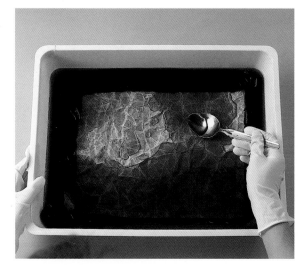

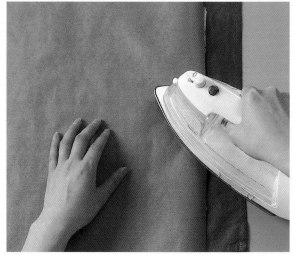

5 Prepare a shallow dye bath with a dark indigo-blue hand dye, following the manufacturer's instructions. Submerge the napkin in the dye, keeping it as flat as possible. When it is the desired colour, rinse it in warm water until the water runs clear. Leave to dry. Repeat with the remaining napkins.

6 Iron the dry napkins between pieces of lining paper or brown paper to remove the wax. Machine wash the napkins to remove any excess dye or grease marks.

DYED GIFT WRAP AND TAGS

This clever technique creates texture as well as colour, as the paper is finely pleated while wet.

Choose a paper with good wet strength, such as Japanese Shoji paper.

YOU WILL NEED
large sheets of white paper
ruler
cold-water dyes
plastic containers for dyes
large household paintbrush
craft knife
cutting mat
watercolour paper or handmade paper
hole punch
ribbon or raffia

1 Fold the paper around the ruler, rolling it over and over along its whole length. The larger the paper, the longer the ruler you will need.

2 Dampen the paper slightly then push it gently up the ruler to make creases.

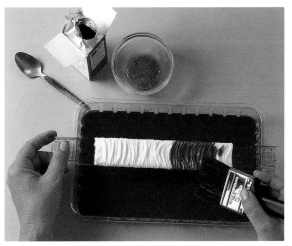

3 Make a dye mix in a suitable container, and soak the paper with dye using a household paintbrush. Experiment, using stronger solutions in places or mixing complementary colours together. ▶

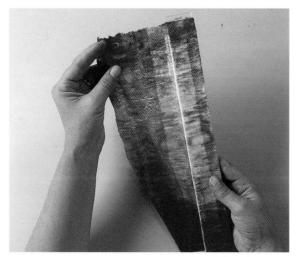

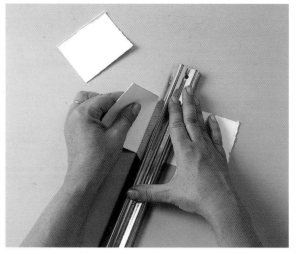

4 Allow to dry at least overnight: if you try to unwrap the paper while it is too wet, it will tear. Gently stretch out the pleats before unwrapping the sheet. Allow to dry thoroughly. Trim any rough edges using a craft knife on a cutting mat if necessary.

5 To make the tags, tear watercolour paper into small rectangles of different shapes and sizes against the edge of a ruler.

6 Mix up small amounts of dye in complementary colours. Dip the torn edges of the paper into the dyes. Allow to dry before dipping again for a stronger colour. Leave some tags white in the middle or submerge the dip-dyed paper thoroughly to colour the tags all over. Complete by making a hole and threading with ribbon or raffia to tie.

Above: Personalize gifts for special friends with colourful hand-dyed wrapping paper and gift tags.

DIP-DYED LAMPSHADE

A plain white linen lampshade can be beautifully dressed up to highlight a colour scheme by simply dipping it in cold-water dyes. The rich colour will bleed slightly into the white linen, creating a lovely feathery effect.

YOU WILL NEED
deep dye bath
cold-water dyes in cherry-red and terracotta
latex gloves
white linen-covered lampshade
absorbent cloth
paper, pencil and ruler
protractor
cherry red stranded embroidery thread (floss)
large-eyed needle
12 red glass beads
12 small beads

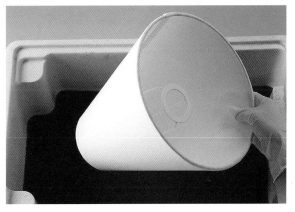

1 Using a deep dye bath, mix up a cherry-red cold-water hand dye. Hold the shade by the base and dip it in the dye so that two-thirds of it is submerged. After a few seconds remove the shade. Repeat the process to intensify the colour. Stand the shade on an absorbent cloth to dry.

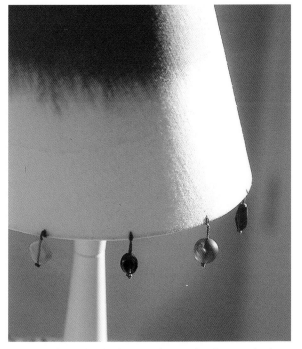

Above: Choose beads that complement the shape and colour of your lampshade.

2 While the shade is still slightly damp, dip the top 5cm/2in in a dye bath containing terracotta dye. Stand the shade on an absorbent cloth to dry, allowing the second colour to bleed through the first. ▶

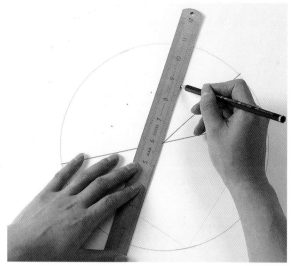

3 Stand the dry shade on a piece of paper and draw around its base. Use a protractor, pencil and ruler to divide the circle into 30° sections.

4 Stand the shade back on the circle and very lightly mark the 30° sections on the bottom of the shade with a pencil.

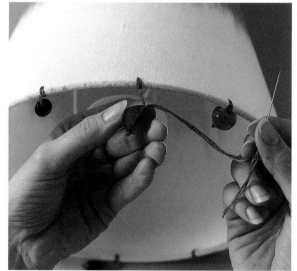

5 Double a piece of embroidery thread (floss) and thread the loop through a needle. Push this through a mark on the lampshade. Take the needle through the loop and pull tight. Thread on a large bead and tie a knot 3cm/1¼in from the base of the shade. If the knot is too small and the bead slips, thread on a small bead before knotting.

6 Take the needle back up through the large bead to hide any untidy ends before neatly cutting the threads. Following the pencil marks in step 4, repeat steps 5 and 6 until you have decorated the entire edge of the lampshade.

NEEDLEPOINT PIN CUSHION

Inspired by Monet's paintings of waterlilies, canvas has been painted and then stitched in random long stitch in silk and wool. It is backed with acid-dyed silk satin and decorated with tassels.

YOU WILL NEED

20cm/8in square of canvas, 10 threads to 2.5cm/1in

plastic sheet

masking tape

medium paintbrush

fabric paints in green, sapphire blue and light pink

iron

acid dyes in bright pinky red, violet, green and reddish blue

white vinegar

dyeing equipment, including latex gloves, metal bowls, measuring spoons, glass jars, stirring rod and thermometer

10g/¼oz white silk 4-ply thread

25cm/10in square white silk satin

50g/2oz 4-ply white Shetland wool (yarn)

felt-tipped pen

ruler

tacking (basting) thread

pins and needles

25cm/10in square of lightweight calico

pins

sewing machine

matching sewing thead

scissors

polyester toy filling (stuffing)

thick cardboard

RECIPE FOR SILK THREAD AND SILK SATIN

40ml/1½fl oz dilute pinky-red dye solution

20ml/4 tsp dilute violet dye solution

40ml/1½fl oz dilute green dye solution

RECIPE FOR SHETLAND WOOL (YARN)

5ml/1 tsp reddish-blue dye solution + 60ml/2fl oz water

10ml/2 tsp green dye solution + 60ml/2fl oz water

5ml/1 tsp violet dye solution + 60ml/2fl oz water

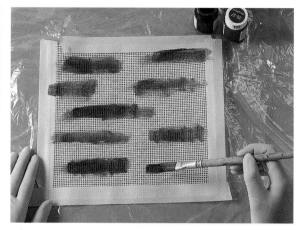

1 Place a 20cm/8in square of canvas on a sheet of plastic and secure in position using masking tape. With light brushstrokes, brush green paint into the fabric evenly over the whole area. Wash the brush thoroughly before changing colours.

2 Add areas of blue, distributing them over the canvas. Cover any remaining areas with light pink. Leave to dry for 24 hours, then iron on the wrong side for a few minutes to fix (set) the dye.

3 Space dye 10g/¼oz medium (4-ply) silk thread, and a 25cm/10in square of silk satin with acid dyes. Use the method for silk described in the techniques section. Use stock solutions of 2.5ml/½ tsp dye in 300ml/½ pint boiling water, diluted by making 20ml/4 tsp dye solution up to 100ml/3½fl oz with water. Iron the silk satin dry and hang the thread up to dry. Space-dye 50g/2oz 4-ply wool (yarn) using the method for wool. Use stock solutions of 2.5ml/½ tsp dye in 300ml/½ pint boiling water. Allow the wool to dry thoroughly before use.

4 Enlarge the template at the back of the book to the required size. Cut it out. Pin the template to the canvas and draw around it using a felt-tipped pen. Stitch over the marked lines using tacking (basting) thread in a contrasting colour.

5 Using two strands of medium (4-ply) silk, fill in the central square of the design area in random long stitch. It should be worked in varying lengths along each row. Work one row from left to right and then the next row from right to left.

6 Using two strands of wool, work the outer shapes in random long stitch, keeping the top and bottom lines and the diagonal lines as straight edges.

7 Tack lightweight calico to the wrong side of the silk to reinforce it, then pin the silk and canvas right sides together. Machine stitch around three sides into the last row of canvas stitches. Trim the seams, clip the corners and turn through. ▶

8 Stuff with polyester toy filling (stuffing) and tuck in the seam allowances along the last side. Do not make the pin cushion too fat. Neatly slipstitch the opening closed, leaving about 0.5cm/¼in open at one end.

9 Make a twisted cord from two strands of wool (yarn) and one of silk. Tie the three ends to a fixed point and twist together. Fold in half, hold the ends and the two lengths will twist together. Knot the ends.

10 Tuck the knotted end of the cord into the small opening. Couch the cord around the pin cushion seam. As you approach the end, re-tie the knot to make it fit exactly and tuck it inside the seam. Stitch closed.

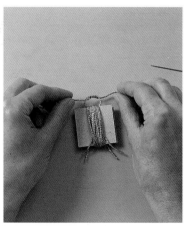

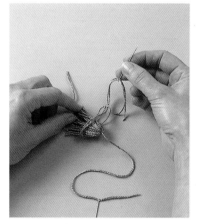

11 To make a tassel, cut two pieces of thick cardboard 4cm/1½in square. Wind silk around the cardboard until the tassel is fat enough, then push a needle threaded with a short length of silk between the two pieces of cardboard at the top and tie tightly into a knot.

12 Cut the loops at the bottom of the tassel between the cardboard. Double another piece of silk and thread a large-eyed needle. Wind around the tassel about 1.5cm/⅝in from the top, thread the ends through the loop and pull tight.

13 Stitch into this thread several times to secure, then take the needle down the centre of the tassel to lose the ends. Make three more tassels. Trim the bottom of each tassel evenly and stitch them to the corners of the pincushion using the tying threads.

QUILTED WALLHANGING

Over a brilliantly coloured patchwork background of space-dyed fabrics, this panel is appliquéd with silk and felt "Indian birds" and completed with decorative hand-stitching in acid-dyed silk.

YOU WILL NEED

1m/40in calico or white cotton fabric, 1.5m/59in wide, plus lightweight calico for backing and batten sleeve

tape measure

scissors

cold-water reactive dyes in red, yellow, lemon yellow, blue, reddish-blue, green

washing soda (sodium carbonate)

dyeing equipment, including latex gloves, plastic bowls, trays, measuring beakers and syringes

iron

cutting mat

ruler

rotary cutter

pins

sewing machine

matching sewing thread

felt interlining

tacking (basting) thread

needle

acid-dyed silk embroidery thread (floss)

four silk and felt birds from Indian Birds project

silk and felt flower made to match birds

44cm/17¾in batten

"D" moulding curtain rings

1 Cut the calico for the hanging into four squares each 50cm/20in, and one rectangle 50 x 100cm/ 20 x 40in. Space-dye each square (each should weigh about 45g/1¾oz) a different colour for the centre triangles. Use the cold-water reactive space-dyed method for pale colours described in the techniques section. The stock solutions are 2.5ml/½ tsp dye in 300ml/½ pint hot water. Dye the rectangle mid-green using the cold-water space-dyed method for deep colours and the same strength stock solutions. Leave to dry and iron flat.

PINK

• 10ml/2 tsp red dye solution + 30ml/1fl oz soda solution + water to make 160ml/5½fl oz

PALE YELLOW – pour each made-up solution on separately

• 10ml/2 tsp yellow dye solution + 20ml/4 tsp soda solution + water to make 80ml/2¾fl oz

• 10ml/2 tsp lemon yellow dye solution + 20ml/4 tsp soda solution + water to make 80ml/2¾fl oz

PALE BLUE – pour each made-up solution on separately

• 10ml/2 tsp blue dye solution + 20ml/4 tsp soda solution + water to make 80ml/2¾fl oz

• 10ml/2 tsp reddish blue dye solution + 20ml/4 tsp soda solution + water to make 80ml/2¾fl oz

PALE GREEN

10ml/2 tsp green + 10ml/2 tsp lemon yellow dye solutions + 30ml/1fl oz soda solution + water to make 160ml/5½fl oz

MID-GREEN

85ml/3fl oz lemon yellow dye solution + 170ml/6fl oz green dye solution + 80ml/2¾fl oz soda solution

2 Cut a 20cm/8 in square of each pale colour. Cut each square diagonally into four triangles. Arrange the triangles to form the pattern shown. Pin and stitch the yellow and blue triangles together with a 1cm/½in seam. Press the seam towards the darker colour.

3 Pin and stitch the pink and green triangles together. Keeping the triangle arrangement correct, sew the pink/green triangles to the blue/yellow triangles with a 1cm/½in seam. Press on the wrong side.

4 Cut strips 7cm/2¾in wide for the border from mid-green calico. From the 7cm/2¾in-wide strip, cut two strips each 17cm/6½in long, cut three strips 37cm/14½in long, and two strips 47cm/18½in long.

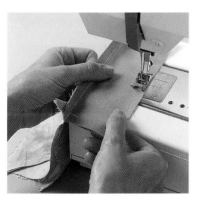

5 With a 1cm/½in seam allowance throughout, stitch one side of each square to one side of each 17cm/6½in strip. Press the seams towards the middle. Between the two panels, stitch a 37cm/14½in strip. Press the square.

6 Stitch 37cm/14½in strips to the top and bottom of the patchwork. Attach the long strips down each side. Check that the patchwork is square and trim if necessary.

7 To make the backing, cut one 47cm/18½in square from lightweight calico and one from felt interlining. Sandwich the interlining between the backing and the patchwork. Pin together from the centre outwards. Quilt using toning thread and stitching along the seamlines, again working from the centre outwards. Tack (baste) the edges and trim.

8 For the edging, cut a 17 x 20cm/6½ x 8in piece of each pale fabric. Join the long sides in the colour order yellow, pink, green and blue. Press the seams to one side, then cut across them to make four strips 4cm/1½in wide. Press under 0.5cm/¼in along one long edge of each strip.

9 With right sides together, match the pink/green seam on the unpressed edge of a length of binding to the centre top of the patchwork. Pin and stitch with a 1cm/½in seam allowance. Press the seam. Repeat at the bottom edge.

10 Fold the binding to the back of the quilt and neatly slipstitch the folded edge in place. Repeat for the bottom edge, then add the sides in the same way. Turn in the raw edges of each short end to align with the quilt edge. Press and neatly stitch in place.

11 Using acid-dyed silk embroidery threads (floss), work a row of decorative running stitch around the inside edge of each triangle. Work several parallel rows along the border. Make up four Indian birds, following the instructions in the Indian Birds project.

12 Pin and stitch a silk and felt bird in the centre of each square. Make a green flower to match the birds using the template at the back of the book. Enlarge the flower to 17cm/6½in wide, and make up in the same way as the Indian birds. Stitch it in place on the quilt centre.

13 To make a batten sleeve, cut a strip of undyed calico 7.5 x 46cm/3 x 18in and press under 1cm/⅜in at each short end. Fold in half lengthways and stitch with a 1cm/½in seam. Press the seam open at the back of the tube. Slipstitch in place on the back of the hanging. Insert the batten and stitch on curtain rings for hanging.

INDIAN BIRDS

These vibrant birds are made from silk satin and dyed felt, sandwiched together and embellished with embroidery and shisha glass. They can be used as appliquéd decorations or stuffed to make pretty hanging ornaments.

YOU WILL NEED
25 x 56cm/10 x 22in silk satin
silk thread
acid dyes for silk in bright pink/red, mid-red, yellow, lemon, blue and red-blue
vinegar
dyeing equipment including latex gloves, plastic trays, metal pans, beakers, syringes and stirring rods
wool/viscose felt
cold-water reactive dyes for viscose in red, yellow, lemon yellow, green, blue and red-blue
washing soda (sodium carbonate)
scissors
bonding powder and/or fusible web
iron and baking parchment
thin cardboard
glue stick
craft knife and cutting mat
pencil
sewing machine
needle
shisha glass
polyester toy filling (stuffing)

1 Dye the silk satin and silk thread with acid dyes using the method described in the techniques section. Each recipe makes enough dye for 32g/1¼oz, which includes 20g/¾oz fine silk thread and a piece of silk satin 25 x 56cm/10 x 22in. Add about 200ml/7fl oz vinegar to the water. All stock solutions are made using 2.5ml/½ tsp dye in 300ml/½ pint boiling water.

RED SILK (ACID DYE)
• 110ml/3¾ fl oz stock pink/red
• 40ml/1½ fl oz stock mid-red

RED FELT (REACTIVE DYE)
• 10ml/2 tsp red dye solution + 30ml/1fl oz soda solution + water to make 200ml/7fl oz

YELLOW SILK (ACID DYE)
• 35ml/1¼ fl oz stock yellow
• 35ml/1¼ fl oz stock lemon

YELLOW FELT (REACTIVE DYE)
• 50ml/2fl oz yellow dye + 30ml/1fl oz soda solution + water to make 100ml/3½ fl oz
• 50ml/2fl oz lemon dye + 30ml/1fl oz soda solution + water to make 100ml/3½ fl oz

GREEN SILK (ACID DYE)
• 85ml/3fl oz stock lemon + 70ml/2¼ fl oz stock blue

GREEN FELT (REACTIVE DYE)
• 80ml/2¾ fl oz green + 20ml/4 tsp yellow dye solutions + 50ml/2fl oz soda solution + water to make 200ml/7fl oz

BLUE SILK (ACID DYE)
• 80ml/2¾ fl oz stock red-blue
• 30ml/1fl oz stock blue

BLUE FELT (REACTIVE DYE)
• 50ml/2fl oz blue dye + 30ml/1fl oz soda solution + water to make 100ml/3½ fl oz
• 50ml/2fl oz red/blue dye + 30ml/1fl oz soda solution + water to make 100ml/3½ fl oz

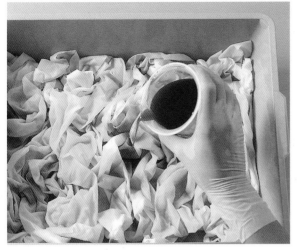

2 Space-dye felt in colours to match the silk using cold water reactive dyes for deep colours as described in the techniques section. The recipes use stock solutions of 2.5ml/½ tsp dye in 300ml/½ pint hot water and will each dye a piece of felt about 50cm/20in square (about 35g/1¼oz). Allow the fabric to dry thoroughly after ironing.

3 Cut a piece of silk large enough to make two or three birds and a piece of felt the same size. Fuse the silk on top of the felt with bonding powder and press with a hot iron, protecting the iron with baking parchment. Repeat for all four colours.

4 Enlarge the templates from the back of the book to 12.5cm/5in. Glue the copy on to thin cardboard and cut out using a craft knife on a cutting mat. Draw around the template on the felt side of the bonded fabrics, turning it over to produce mirror images for half the birds.

5 Stitch the outline in stab stitch or free machine embroidery following the pencil line. Use a shiny bobbin thread in the machine as this will show on the right side.

6 To add contrasting panels on the bird's body and wing, bond fusible web to the wrong side of various colours of silk. Draw around the templates on to the paper side of the webbing and accurately cut out. Peel off the paper and pin each shape in place. ▶

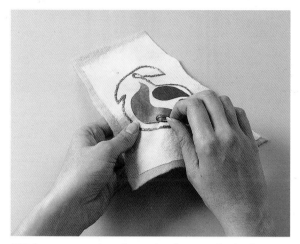

7 Iron contrasting shapes in place on the background piece. Protect the plate of the iron with baking parchment. Using contrasting silk thread, work chain stitch around the outline of each bird and the wing and head. Add rows of running stitch detail.

8 To attach the shisha, sew two threads across it and two more at right angles to the first pair, to make a cross. Make four diagonal stitches across the corners of the cross, to make a frame. Starting on the outside edge, loop around the frame and work a tiny stitch into the fabric with the needle pointing clockwise. This forms a half Cretan stitch. Repeat around the mirror edge, then chain stitch around the edge.

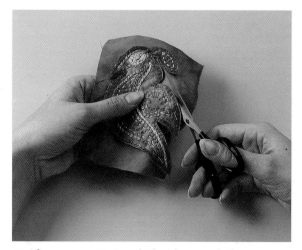

9 If you are not using shisha glass, work the eye in a chain stitch spiral. When the embroidery is complete, cut around the shape using sharp scissors. At this stage, the birds can be applied to the wallhanging.

10 For a hanging bird, make a short twisted cord from embroidery silk. Form a loop and stitch the ends behind the top of the bird's head. Oversew a pair of mirror-image birds together. Stuff softly with toy filling (stuffing) before the stitching is complete.

PAISLEY PELMET

Triangular flags, encrusted with beading and embroidery and finished with tassels, form a distinctive window dressing: team the pelmet with plain curtains dyed to match or use it alone to decorate a small window.

YOU WILL NEED

0.5m/½yd white cotton poplin, 1.5m/59in wide
cold-water reactive dyes in yellow and lemon yellow
washing soda (sodium carbonate)
dyeing equipment including latex gloves, plastic trays, glass jars,
measuring beakers and syringes
small pieces of silk and cotton textured fabrics, including raw silk,
satin, brocade and cotton velvet
tape measure
scissors
pencil
ruler
bonding powder and fusible bonding web
unwoven pelmet stiffener
pins
baking parchment
iron
glue stick
thin cardboard
craft knife
cutting mat
sewing machine
machine embroidery thread (floss) in shades of yellow and gold
hand embroidery thread (floss) including yellow silk, viscose floss
and gold thread
embroidery, beading and sewing needles
rotary cutter
yellow and gold beads
shisha glass (optional)
matching sewing thread
stiff cardboard
length of 3 x 0.8cm/1¼ x ⅜in wooden batten to fit across window

1 Space-dye the poplin yellow using the cold water reactive dye method for deep colours described in the techniques section. Use stock solutions of 2.5ml/½ tsp dye in 300ml/½ pint hot water. Dye small pieces of textured fabrics in two other shades of yellow. Weigh the fabrics when dry and dye half with each recipe.

YELLOW RECIPE FOR 100G/3½ OZ MAIN FABRIC
• 150ml/5fl oz yellow dye solution + 60ml/2fl oz soda solution
• 150ml/5fl oz lemon yellow dye solution + 60ml/2fl oz soda solution

GOLDEN YELLOW RECIPE FOR 30G/1OZ MIXED FABRICS
• 120ml/4fl oz yellow dye solution + 60ml/2fl oz soda solution

LEMON YELLOW RECIPE FOR 30G/1OZ MIXED FABRICS
• 100ml/3½fl oz yellow dye solution + 60ml/2fl oz soda solution

2 Cut a strip of yellow poplin 20cm/8in wide to fit the length of the batten plus 3cm/1¼in for turnings. Set aside. Mark out a strip 10cm/4in wide for the front of the batten casing, and as many 12 x 20cm/4¾ x 8in right-angled triangles as you will need to fit across the window.

3 Bond the fabric for the flags and casing strip front to the pelmet stiffener using bonding powder. Sprinkle the powder over the stiffener, pin the poplin over the top and cover with baking parchment to protect the iron. Use a hot iron to bond the fabrics. Allow to cool.

4 Bond fusible bonding web to the wrong side of small pieces of textured fabrics. Enlarge the paisley template from the back of the book to 4cm/1½in long. Glue on to thin cardboard and cut out. Draw around the template on to the paper backing and cut out the fabric shapes.

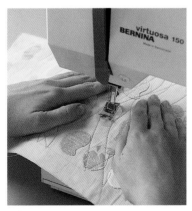

5 Bond the shapes to the flags and central 3cm/1¼in of the casing strip, avoiding the pencil outlines. Using machine embroidery threads (floss) in a range of colours, stitch gentle curved lines over and around the paisley shapes.

6 Enhance the flags with hand embroidery in yellow silk and gold thread, using chain stitch to surround the shapes and cable chain to stitch curvy lines.

7 Cut out the flags and trim the casing strip to 3cm/1¼in wide using a rotary cutter. Add yellow and gold beads and stitch on shisha glass to catch the light if desired.

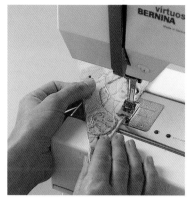

8 Cut an equal number of triangles from spare poplin. Pin each decorated flag to a backing piece and machine stitch around the edge with a small, narrow zigzag.

9 Fold the reserved batten casing in half lengthways and press. Turn under and press 1.5cm/⅝in at each short end. Pin the decorated casing strip 3mm/⅛in from the foldline and stitch with a narrow zigzag.

10 Pin the casing loosely around the batten. Remove the batten and stitch along the pinned line.

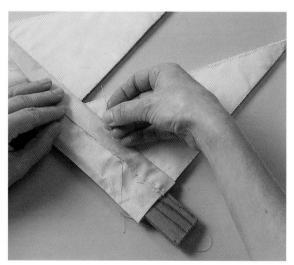

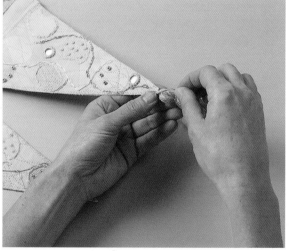

11 Stitch the flags securely to the casing, just under the previous seam. Press the raw edges of the casing up, insert the batten and slipstitch the raw edges in place.

12 For the tassels, cut two pieces of thick cardboard 7cm/2¾in square. Wind silk around the cards, then push a needle and thread between them at the top and tie tightly. Cut the loops at the bottom between the cards. Wind double thread around each tassel about 1.5cm/⅝in from the top, thread the ends through the loop, pull tight and tie. Trim the bottom. Stitch one to the end of each flag.

DIP-DYED ALBUM COVER

Japanese paper is ideal for this technique as it needs to be thin but strong. Experiment with variations, such as dipping the folded paper into plain water before the dye for a soft effect, or waiting until the colour is dry and then re-dipping for a stronger colour.

YOU WILL NEED
Japanese Shoji paper
craft knife
steel rule
cutting mat
bulldog clips
hand dye or watercolour inks in three colours
small containers for dye or inks
iron
thin cardboard
spray adhesive
paper for the album pages
glue stick
pencil
rotating hole punch
decorative ribbon

1 Cut two sheets of Shoji paper 3cm/1¼in larger all around than the finished album cover. Fold each one into an accordion.

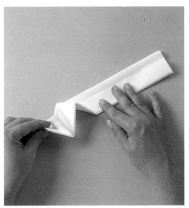

2 Now fold the accordion up into another accordion (you can do this at an angle to make a triangular shape, or keep to a square shape). Clamp with bull-dog clips.

3 Mix up some hand dyes in strong solutions or place some watercolour inks in small containers. Three colours work best. Dip just one corner of the paper into the dye at a time.

4 You may wish to let the colours blend into each other, or allow them to dry before continuing with the next colour.

▶

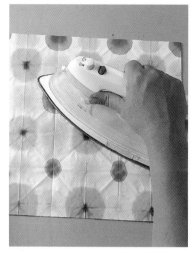

5 When the paper is completely dry, open it out and iron it gently with a dry, cool iron to flatten the creases.

6 Cut the front and back of the album out of thin cardboard. Glue the paper to the thin cardboard, then trim the corners diagonally before folding and gluing down the flaps.

7 Cut two sheets of paper a little smaller than the covers. Glue the paper to the inside of each cover to hide the flaps.

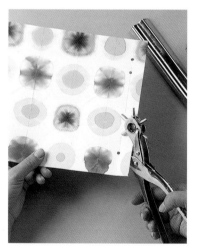

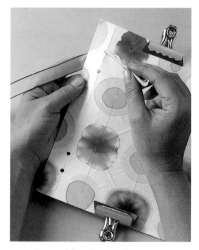

8 Mark the position for the holes with a pencil on the album covers. These should be at least 2cm/¾in in from the back edge and the top and bottom of the page. Make the holes with a rotating hole punch.

9 Collate the album pages and hold them together with bulldog clips. Mark the position for the holes and punch.

10 To finish, tie the covers and pages together with decorative ribbon.

SILK TABLERUNNER

Carefully pressed, even pleats result in a design that combines the spontaneity of tie-dyeing with restrained formality. It is perfectly set off by the wonderful papery texture of wild silk.

YOU WILL NEED
lilac silk dupion, hand-washed to remove any dressing
iron
ruler
scissors
fine cord or string
latex gloves
dye bath
blue hand dye
salt (if necessary)
pins
needle
matching sewing thread

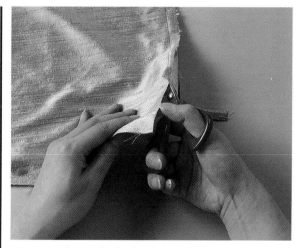

1 Iron the washed silk while still damp. Cut to the size required for the runner (the length measurement should include the fringe), allowing 4.5cm/1¾in wastage on each side.

2 Pleat the fabric concertina-fashion, making each pleat about 3cm/1¼in wide. If your runner is very long the pleats may become unmanageable, so you may wish to make the pleats parallel with the long sides.

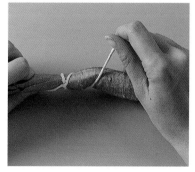

3 Using fine cord or string, bind the fabric tightly along the length of the pleats, spacing the bindings about 7.5cm/3in apart. Start with the central binding and work out towards the edges of the fabric.

4 Prepare a dye bath large enough to allow the fabric to move freely. Dampen the tied cloth before placing it in the bath to help ensure an even colour. Dye the fabric according to the manufacturer's instructions. ▶

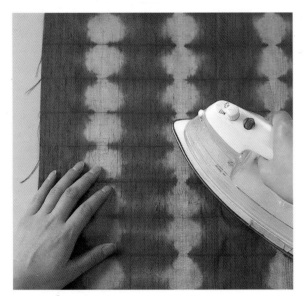

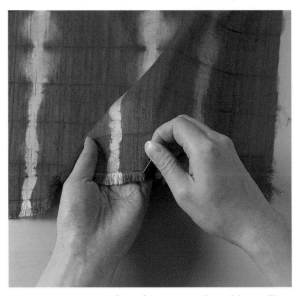

5 When the fabric is the desired colour, remove it from the dye and rinse it under cold water until the water runs clear. Then remove the bindings and hand-wash the silk to remove any excess dye. Iron flat while still damp.

6 Using a pin, make a fringe at each end by pulling out the weft threads until you have a frayed edge about 4cm/1½in deep. Fold the cloth in half to ensure that it is square, and trim away 2.5cm/1in from each long side.

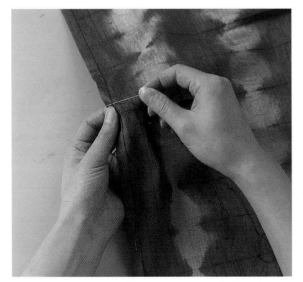

7 Turn over and press a 1cm/½in double hem on each side. Hand sew, picking up as little cloth as you can with the needle so that the hemming will not show on the front of the runner.

8 Finally, trim the ends of the fringe at each end if necessary to neaten them.

PATCHWORK TOY BAG

This brightly coloured bag makes a safe place to keep small toys. Two dyeing methods have been used: with each method, dye extra fabric and choose the best pieces for the patchwork.

YOU WILL NEED

white cotton lawn, 1.5m/59in wide

2.5m/2¾yd cotton piping cord

cold-water reactive dyes in red, green and violet

salt

washing soda (sodium carbonate)

dyeing equipment including latex gloves, plastic trays, measuring beakers, jam jars, plastic bag, clothes pegs (pins), pepperpots (pepper shakers) or muslin squares and household paintbrush

scissors

pencil and ruler

rotary cutter and cutting mat

pins

sewing machine

matching sewing thread

large safety pin

DEEP PINK

400ml/14fl oz red dye solution + 200ml/7fl oz soda solution

1 Space-dye at least four pieces of lawn by the pepperpot (pepper shaker) method using red, green and violet (see Techniques). Dye 1m/40in lawn and the piping cord deep pink by the reactive space-dyeing method for deep colours. The recipe given is for about 150g/5½oz fabric and cord. Use a stock solution of 5ml/1 tsp dye in 300ml/½ pint hot water. From pepperpot fabric, cut 24 squares each 12cm/4¾in. From deep pink, cut 24 squares, and two pieces 62 x 42cm/24½ x 16½in for the lining.

2 Using 1cm/½in seams, stitch the squares together in rows, alternating the colours. Press the seams to one side. Make 12 rows of four squares each.

3 Stitch six rows together for each side, alternating the colours. Trim the extra fabric from the corners and press the seams to one side.

4 With right sides together, pin and stitch both long sides of the lining pieces together with a 1cm/½in seam to make a tube. Press the seams open. ▶

5 Repeat with the two patch-work pieces, leaving a 3cm/1¼in gap in each side seam 7cm/2¾in from the top. Press the seams open.

6 With right sides together and side seams matching, slip one tube inside the other and stitch together around the top, through two layers of fabric. Turn through, press and topstitch on the outside of the bag.

7 Form the casing for the cord with two rows of machine stitching parallel to the top edge and 7cm/2¾in and 10cm/4in below it.

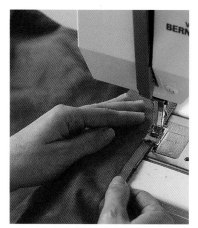

8 Turn the bag inside out and machine stitch the bottom through all four layers of fabric. This prevents the lining slipping when the bag is in use. Stitch again to reinforce the seam. Trim the bottom edges and neaten with a zigzag stitch. Turn through.

9 Cut the piping cord in half. Attach a safety pin to the end of one piece and thread through a side opening, around the casing and out through the same opening.

10 Repeat with the second piece of cord through the second side opening. Knot all of the ends to finish.

TEA-DYED HOT WATER BOTTLE COVER

The fabric used for this cuddly hot water bottle cover was cut from an old blanket that
had seen better days. With an appealing teddy bear motif subtly coloured with tea,
it will cheer up bedtime on the frostiest night.

YOU WILL NEED

tea bags	scissors
dye baths	brown ribbon 1.5cm/⅝in wide
old blanket or wool fabric,	sewing machine
pre-washed	matching sewing thread
iron	satin bias binding (optional)
pressing cloth	2m/2yd fine brown cord
brown hand dye	safety pin
hot water bottle	fabric marker
pencil	stranded embroidery
paper	thread (floss)
tailor's chalk	needle
	tiny buttons

1 Steep two or three teabags in hot water in a small dye bath until the solution is quite strong. Immerse the fabric for the teddy motif in the tea. Agitate until you are happy with the colour, re-dyeing if necessary. Dry the fabric and press under a damp cloth.

2 Dye a larger piece of fabric for the cover in brown hand dye in the same way. Dry and press as before.

3 Make a paper template for the cover using the hot water bottle. Fold the fabric in half and place the template on top. Draw around it with tailor's chalk. Cut out a rectangular back and front large enough to fit the bottle. ▶

4 To make a casing for the cord, on the wrong side of the front and back, sew a length of ribbon across each cover piece about 5cm/2in below the top edge.

5 Using a 1cm/½in seam, stitch the back and front together. Leave a gap in the stitching at each end of the casing for the cord to pass through. Bind the top edge of the cover with ribbon or satin bias binding.

6 Cut the cord in half and use a safety pin to thread one length through a side opening, around the casing and out through the same opening. Knot the two ends. Repeat with the second piece of cord through the second side opening.

7 Copy the teddy motif at the back of the book and enlarge it to a suitable size. Draw around the template on the tea-dyed fabric using a fabric marker. Draw in the features.

8 Embroider the features using stranded embroidery thread (floss). Add small buttons for eyes.

9 Cut out the teddy face and slipstitch it to the front of the cover, taking care not to catch the back of the cover in the stitching.

SILK CUSHION

All the fabrics used to make this luxurious cushion are dyed together, but four different shades of dye are used simultaneously, to create a very rich effect. The various textured fabrics are assembled in a crazy patchwork design and are decorated with lace and beads.

YOU WILL NEED

0.5m/½yd white silk satin, pre-washed
small amounts of textured silks, cotton and viscose fabrics,
including taffeta, beaded silk, brocade and cotton velvet
short lengths of cotton lace
2m/2yd viscose cord
cold-water reactive dyes in blue, black, green and lemon yellow
washing soda (sodium carbonate)
dyeing equipment including latex gloves, plastic tray, jam jars,
stirring rods, measuring beakers, plastic bag and
clothes pegs (pins)
iron and pressing cloth
tape measure
lightweight calico
scissors
ruler
pencil
pins
tacking (basting) thread
needle
matching sewing thread
sewing machine
35cm/13½in zipper fastener
40cm/16in square cushion pad

RECIPE FOR 100G/3½OZ FABRIC

• 50ml/2fl oz blue dye solution + 25ml/5 tsp soda solution

• 50ml/2fl oz black dye solution + 25ml/5 tsp soda solution

• 40ml/1½fl oz green + 20ml/4 tsp lemon yellow dye solutions +
30ml/1fl oz soda solution

• 25ml/5 tsp green + 25ml/5 tsp blue dye solutions + 25ml/5 tsp
soda solution

1 Space-dye the fabrics and cord using the cold-water reactive dye method for deep colours described in the techniques section. Weigh the fabrics and adjust the recipe if necessary. Use solutions of 5ml/1 tsp dye in 300ml/½ pint hot water.

2 When the dyeing is complete, rinse and wash the fabrics and iron dry. Do not spin-dry silk or it will crease. Allow the fabric to air before starting. ▶

3 To line the cushion front and back, cut two squares of lightweight calico (muslin) each 45cm/18in. Mark the size of the cushion on one square with a pencil. This will leave a 2.5cm/1in allowance all round. Mark a 5cm/2in border inside the square, on both sides of the calico.

4 Cut a 43cm/17in square of satin to form the back of the cushion, and tack (baste) to the unmarked piece of calico. Trim the calico to size. Cut four strips of satin 7.5 x 44cm/3 x 17½in and reserve for the borders.

5 Cut pieces of dyed fabric and position them in a random design in the centre square of the cushion front. Press under 0.5cm/¼in along the edges of the lighter fabrics and lap them over the heavier ones. Overlap the borders by at least 1cm/½in. Pin each piece in place.

6 Insert pieces of lace into some seams at random, ensuring that the raw ends are hidden under adjacent pieces of fabric. Neatly slipstitch the patches to the calico backing, working from the centre outwards. Ensure that the patches remain flat and that there are no gaps.

7 Place border strips, right sides down, on two opposite sides and stitch along the marked line with a 1cm/½in seam allowance. Press the strips outwards and tack along the outside edge. Repeat with the remaining border strips.

8 Trim the front to 43cm/17in square and press under a 1.5cm/⅝in seam allowance along one side of the front and back. Insert the zipper fastener. Pin and stitch the remaining sides, leaving a 0.5cm/¼in gap near the zipper. Turn through and press. Slipstitch the cord to the seamline and beside the zip on the front, inserting the knotted ends into the small gap. Slipstitch closed.

LILAC DEVORE BLIND

Devoré velvet is made by etching a design into the fabric using a medium that destroys the silk pile, leaving the backing intact. Using it as a blind makes the most of this lovely fabric, as the light passes through the etched pattern.

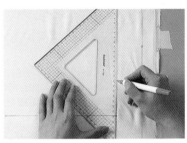

1 Enlarge the design at the back of the book to the required size. Outline it with a black pen, so that it is visible through the velvet. Cut the velvet to size, allowing 2cm/¾in wastage all round. Tape it, pile side down, to the work surface. Using a fabric marker, mark up the blind with a grid to fit the template.

2 Place the design template underneath the fabric and trace it with the fabric marker. Move the template and repeat until the whole grid has been filled in.

3 Stretch the fabric on to a painting frame with the pile upwards, using fine-pointed flat-headed pins.

4 Go over the design with fabric etching medium, following the manufacturer's instructions. Keep your movements fast to prevent the lines becoming too thick (practise on a spare piece of fabric first). ▶

5 Dry the etching medium with a hairdryer, especially if you have to reposition the fabric on the frame, as this may cause smudging. Once the medium is dry, iron the fabric on the wrong side using a cool iron. Trim away the wastage around the edge so that the fabric is the exact size of the blind.

6 Place the fabric in water to reveal the devoré pattern, rubbing the surface if necessary to remove the unwanted fibres. Dye the blind to the required shade while the fabric is still damp, using hand dye and following the manufacturer's instructions.

7 When the velvet is dry, open up a piece of bias binding long enough to run down the side of the blind and stitch it to the wrong side.

8 Fold the binding over to the right side of the blind and topstitch close to the edge of the binding. Trim the top and bottom of the bound edge level with the top and bottom of the blind. Repeat on the other side.

9 Bind the bottom, leaving 1cm/½in extra at each end of the binding. Fold this in before topstitching to give neat corners.

10 Complete the blind using a roller blind kit. You may wish to stick the blind with masking tape first, to make sure that it is straight, before sticking it permanently.

MATERIALS

*Natural fabrics are used for all the dyeing techniques
described in this book.*

BEADS – Use these for decoration.

BONDING POWDER (FUSIBLE WEB)
This is used to bond two fabrics
together with heat.

DYES – Acid dyes are used for
wool and silk, cold-water reactive
dyes for cotton, viscose and silk.
Special fabric paints and printing
inks are also available.

FABRICS – These include cotton
poplin, calico (muslin), lawn, silk
satin, silk mixtures, wool, velvet
and viscose felt. All cotton fabrics,
except velvet, should be machine-
washed at 60°C/140°F, then dried.
Unless they are dirty, wool and
silk should be dampened in warm
water with washing-up liquid
added before dyeing.

NON-WOVEN INTERFACING –
Available in a range of weights,
including pelmet weight.

POLYESTER TOY STUFFING – Light
and resilient, this can be used for
stuffing small shapes.

SALT – Common salt is needed for
some reactive dyeing methods, and
is used with machine dyes.

THREADS (FLOSS) AND YARNS –
These include stranded thread
(floss), viscose floss, gold
embroidery thread, wool and silk
yarn, and cotton threads. Try

dyeing silk and wool thread for
embroidery, or cotton lace,
viscose cord and cotton or viscose
fringing for sewing projects.

UREA – Although not essential,
this is used in solution to help dissolve the dye in strong solutions. It
also allows greater dye penetration
when spray-dyeing and fabric
painting with reactive dyes.

WASHING SODA (SODIUM CARBON-
ATE) – Use a solution of washing
soda to fix reactive dyes. Dissolve
100g/3½oz washing soda crystals in
500ml/18fl oz boiling water. Stir
well and allow to cool.

WASHING-UP (DISHWASHING) LIQ-
UID – Used for soaking or wet-
ting-out fabric and threads before
dyeing, and for setting cottons. A
neutral pH detergent is preferable,
especially when fixing cotton in
hot water as it prevents any
unfixed dye being picked up by
another part of the cotton fabric.

WHITE VINEGAR – This is used to
fix acid dyes.

*Opposite: urea (1), dyes (2), washing
soda (3), salt (4), machine embroidery
threads (floss) (5), fabric printing inks
(6), white vinegar (7), fabric paints
(8), beads (9), cotton lace (10), piping
cord (11), hand embroidery threads
(floss) (12), fabrics (13), wax beads
(14), shisha glass and buttons (15).*

EQUIPMENT

Essential equipment is listed below.

BAKING PARCHMENT – Protect your ironing board with a cloth while ironing fabric dry. Use baking parchment to protect the iron.

DYE BATHS – Use plastic bowls, trays or margarine pots for cold-water dyeing; metal bowls, empty, cleaned food cans or old saucepans for acid dyeing.

FABRIC MARKERS – Choose ones that fade or wash out of fabric.

GLASS JARS WITH LIDS – Use when making and storing dye solutions.

GLOVES AND MASKS – Protect your hands to avoid staining skin. Avoid inhaling powdered dye or spray: wear a mask if necessary.

KNIVES AND SCISSORS – Use a rotary cutting set for accurately cutting fabrics and a craft knife for templates. Use a separate pair of scissors for cardboard and paper.

MASKING TAPE – Use this to hold fabric steady.

MEASURING TOOLS – Use a tape measure, ruler or set (t-) square for measuring fabric.

PAINTBRUSHES – You will need a 2.5cm/1in household brush as well as fine artist's brushes.

PENCIL AND PAPER – Use to make templates and mark fabric.

PEPPERPOTS – Use pepperpots (pepper shakers) or muslin squares.

PLASTIC BAGS AND CLOTHES PEGS (PINS) – Use these to cover dye baths when using reactive dyes.

PRINTING PAD – Cut a piece of blanket to fit into a dish. Use wood offcuts for printing blocks.

STIRRING RODS – Used for mixing dye solutions, these can be glass or plastic rods or lengths of bamboo.

THERMOMETER – Fasten to a stirring rod with rubber bands to protect it while stirring a solution.

WEIGHING AND MEASURING – Use measuring spoons for dye powders, calibrated beakers and syringes for measuring liquids, scales for dry fabrics, salt, soda and urea.

Opposite: dye bath (1), jug (2), measuring cylinder (3), scales (4), blanket (5), plastic bags (6), masking tape (7), spoons (8), syringe (9), clothes pegs (pins) (10), tailor's chalk (11), printing blocks (12), gloves (13), dust mask (14), stirring rod (15), thermometer (16), jam jar (17), rotary cutting set (18), baking parchment (19), rule (20), meauring beakers (21), spray bottle (22), muslin (23), sandpaper (24), bonding powder (25), pepperpots (pepper shakers) (26), craft knife (27), paintbrush (28), fabric marker (29), scissors (30).

BASIC TECHNIQUES

A few basic safety rules should be followed when working with dyes and fabric paints. Label all solutions and powders and keep them away from children and animals. Do not eat or drink while using dyes, and wash your hands before handling food. If you spill dye powder, sweep up as much as possible before washing with plenty of water. Blot up spilt dye solution with newspaper, then wash down. Dye stains can usually be removed from hard surfaces with neat household cleaner or diluted bleach.

PREPARING SODA SOLUTION AND COLD-WATER REACTIVE DYE

When space-dyeing with cold water dyes, it is best to use no more than three to four times the volume of liquid to the weight of the fabric.

To dye 100g/3½oz fabric, use up to 400ml/14fl oz total liquid (including soda solution and water), though thick fabric may need more liquid. Reactive dyes are fixed with washing soda (sodium carbonate).

1 To make a soda solution, dissolve 100g/3½oz washing soda crystals in 500ml/18fl oz boiling water. Stir well and allow to cool.

2 To make a stock dye solution, pour 300ml/½ pint water into a glass jar, mark the level and pour the water away.

3 Measure 2.5ml/½ tsp dye powder into the jar. Add a few drops of cold water and stir to a paste.

4 Pour hot water (not more than 60°C/140°F) into the jar up to the mark and stir thoroughly until the dye is dissolved. The mixture will remain usable for about a week but will gradually lose strength.

COLD-WATER REACTIVE SPACE-DYED METHOD FOR PALE COLOURS

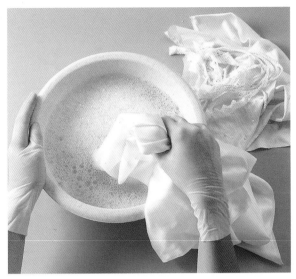

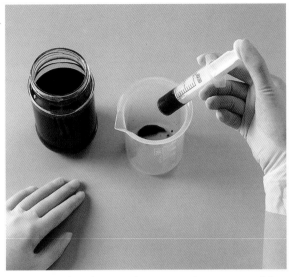

1 Weigh the fabric to be dyed, then soak in warm water with a little washing-up (dishwashing) liquid added for at least 30 minutes. Squeeze out the excess water and crumple the fabric in the dye bath.

2 For each colour used, measure the amount of dye solution needed with a syringe and pour into a measuring beaker. Refer to the recipe, and add the amount of water required.

3 Measure the soda solution (sodium carbonate) needed and pour into the beaker containing dye solution. Once this has been added, the dye solution must be used fairly quickly, as it will lose strength within a couple of hours.

4 Pour the solutions carefully over the fabric in the dye bath. (Dye baths for cold water reactive dye methods can be plastic.) Try to cover all white parts, but do not stir or the colours may become muddy.

5 Leave for at least one hour at room temperature, then rinse thoroughly until the water runs clear. Wash in hot water with a little washing-up liquid added, then rinse again. Allow the fabric to dry partially and then iron completely dry. It is ready for use after airing.

COLD-WATER REACTIVE SPACE-DYED METHOD FOR DEEP COLOURS

1 If very strong solutions of dye are needed, you may prefer to make them up in chemical water. This helps the dye dissolve but does not affect the colour or depth of shade. To make chemical water, weigh out 120g/4oz urea and make up to 1 litre/1¾ pints with hot water. Stir well and allow to cool. Make the dye into a paste with cold water, then make up to 300ml/½ pint with chemical water.

2 Spread out the fabric in a plastic dye bath. The more crumpled the fabric is, the greater the patterning will be.

3 Measure the chemical dye solution according to the recipe and add the soda solution (sodium carbonate) as before. Pour the solutions carefully over the fabric in the dye bath, trying to cover all white parts. Do not stir unless asked to do so, as three-colour mixtures can become especially muddy.

4 If the dye bath or container has a lid, put it on securely. Otherwise put the dye bath in a plastic bag and seal with clothes pegs (pins). Leave undisturbed for 24–48 hours, then remove the fabric and rinse thoroughly until the water is clear.

5 Wash in hot water with a little washing-up liquid added and then rinse again until the water runs clear. Allow fabrics to dry partially, then iron dry and air before using.

MAKING A SOLUTION FOR USE WITH ACID DYES

Acid dyes will work only with the addition of an acid (such as white vinegar) to the dye bath. They are available as powder, which must be dissolved in boiling water, or in liquid form. They can be used on wool, alpaca, angora, cashmere and silk, but not on cotton or linen. The resulting colours are light-fast and will not bleach with washing. Always use a metal dye bath when working with acid dyes.

1 To make up a stock acid dye solution, pour 300ml/½ pint water into a jar, mark the level and pour it away. Measure 2.5ml/½ tsp dye powder into the jar and stir to a paste with cold water.

2 Add boiling water while stirring until the 300ml/ ½ pint mark is reached. This mixture will remain stable for several months.

SPACE-DYEING WOOL WITH ACID DYES

1 Weigh the material to be dyed. Soak it in warm water with a little washing-up (dish-washing) liquid added for at least 30 minutes. Squeeze out excess water gently, without wringing or rubbing. Crumple fabrics and place in the bottom of a metal pan, but lay skeins of yarn so that a maximum amount of the surface is showing.

2 For each colour to be used, measure the volume of stock dye solution and pour it into a measuring beaker. Add any water necessary to make it up to the volume required. Pour the dyes carefully over the wool, aiming to cover all the white parts, and leave for 10 minutes. Use a maximum of 1½–2 times the volume of dye to fabric and yarn.

3 Use 1–3 times the volume of white vinegar to fabric, (allow more for deep colours). Add the vinegar to water and pour down the side of the dye bath. It will barely cover the fabric. Heat gently and bring slowly to the boil. All the dye should stay on the yarn: if the liquid is not clear, add extra vinegar. Simmer for 30 minutes. Remove from the heat and allow to cool slightly. Rinse in hot water, adding cold water to cool the wool gradually. Squeeze out excess water and hang to dry.

SPACE-DYEING SILK WITH ACID DYES

Acid-dyeing produces much faster colours in silk than reactive dyeing. The dye bath is heated to fix the dyes, but the silk must not boil or it will harden and crease badly. Using a water bath may make it easier to control the temperature.

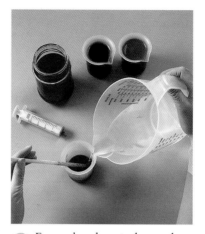

1 Weigh the silk then soak in warm water with a little washing-up (dishwashing) liquid added for at least 30 minutes. Squeeze out excess water and place fabric or yarn in the bottom of a metal pan.

2 For each colour to be used, measure the volume of stock dye solution and pour it into a measuring beaker. Add any water necessary to make it up to the volume required. Refer to the specific recipe.

3 Pour the dyes carefully over the silk. The total volume of dye should not be more than 1½–2 times the weight of the fabric or yarn: a larger amount may be used, but a flatter, more even colour will result.

4 Dye tends to colour silk quite fast, so make sure that all the white parts are covered. Leave for 10 minutes.

5 Use 1–3 times the volume of white vinegar to fabric, using more for deeper colours. Add the white vinegar to water and pour down the side of the dye bath so that it barely covers the fabric or yarn.

6 Heat the dye bath slowly to no more than 85°C/185°F, using a thermometer to check the temperature constantly. After 30 minutes at this temperature, remove from the heat and allow to cool completely before rinsing.

FABRIC PAINTING WITH REACTIVE DYES

1 Make 300ml/½ pint soda solution up to 1.5 litres/ 2¾ pints with water and immerse the prepared dry fabric for 10 minutes. Remove and allow to dry. Make up a solution of chemical water by dissolving 120g/4oz urea in 1 litre/1¾ pints hot water.

2 Measure 2.5ml/½ tsp dye into a small beaker. Add a few drops of cold water and stir to a paste. Add the chemical water slowly while stirring to make up the volume to 100ml/3½fl oz. Repeat for each colour used.

3 Arrange the fabric on a large plastic sheet to protect the work surface. Paint on the first colour with large brush strokes, evenly spaced over the surface. Wash the brush clean in cold water and allow to dry before changing colours.

4 Paint the subsequent colours evenly in the spaces, allowing some overlapping of the dye solutions. A smaller brush will give a more delicate effect and the dye solutions can be made up weaker if required.

5 Place a second sheet of plastic over the fabric and roll up around a length of plastic piping. Additional pieces of fabric can be rolled on top.

6 Put the roll inside another plastic bag and seal. Leave for 24–48 hours, then remove the fabric and rinse in cold water until it runs clear. Wash in hot soapy water and rinse again. Allow the fabric to dry partially, then iron dry.

SPRAY DYEING AND MASKING

The best results are obtained on
fine dry fabric, but do not be
afraid to experiment with different
types and weights of fabric. Do
not use more than three colours,
or they will become muddy.

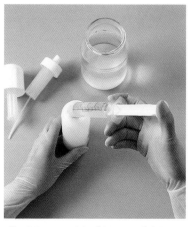

1 If possible, work outdoors.
Hang the fabric from a clothes
line and weight the bottom. If you
have to work indoors, mask the
work area carefully by taping
layers of newspaper to the
surrounding walls. Tape the fabric
to the newspaper.

2 Measure 2.5ml/½ tsp dye
powder into a glass jar and stir
to a paste with a little cold water.
Make up to 300ml/½ pint with
chemical water and stir well.
Ordinary water at 60°C/140°F
may be used, but dyes will spread
more when sprayed.

3 Measure 20ml/4 tsp of this
solution into a spray bottle
and add an equal amount of soda
solution. Repeat steps 2–3 for
each colour used.

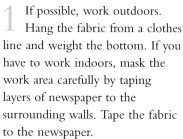

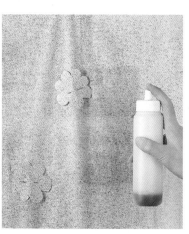

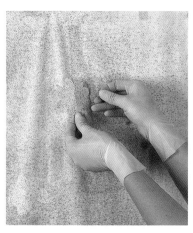

4 Spray the fabric lightly,
allowing a few minutes' rest
between colours to let the colour
spread. Spray evenly over the
whole piece or concentrate
colours in particular areas.

5 Areas may be masked by
pinning paper shapes to the
fabric after one colour has been
sprayed and then spraying up to
two more colours.

6 Remove the masks and allow
the fabric to dry thoroughly,
preferably overnight. Press with a
hot iron. Wash the fabric in hot
soapy water, allow to dry then
iron again.

PEPPERPOT (PEPPER SHAKER) METHOD WITH REACTIVE DYES

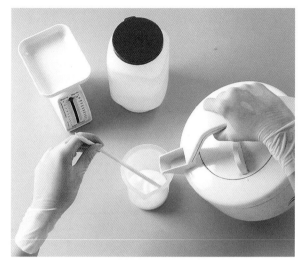

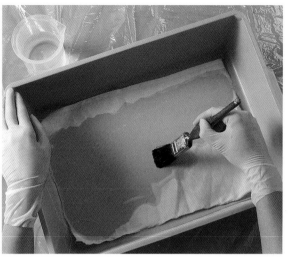

1 Make a salt solution by dissolving 25g/1oz salt in 100ml/3½fl oz hot water. Allow to cool, then measure 25ml/5 tsp salt solution and 40ml/1½fl oz soda solution into a jar. Make the mixture up to 150ml/5fl oz with cold water.

2 This method works best with fine fabrics, but interesting results are also obtained on heavier fabrics such as calico. Cut a piece of dry fabric to fit into the bottom of a deep plastic tray and paint with the salt and soda solution until damp but not too wet.

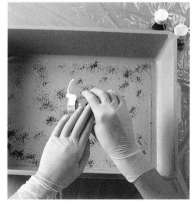

3 Put small amounts of up to three powdered cold-water reactive dyes into pepperpots (pepper shakers). (If these are not available, put each dye into a small square of doubled muslin and gather up the edges with your fingers.)

4 Very carefully, shake dye from the pepperpot or muslin bundle on to the fabric, a small amount at a time. Leave for a minute between applications, as the colour will develop quite quickly. Be very sparing with the dye.

5 Leave for at least 30 minutes to one hour, then remove the fabric from the dye bath and rinse in cold water until it runs clear. Wash in hot soapy water, then rinse again and squeeze out the excess water. Iron the fabric dry.

TIE DYEING

The principle of this technique is to bind areas of the cloth tightly so that they resist the dye. Many patterns can be achieved by simply folding, gathering, sewing or pinching the cloth, using raffia, rubber bands, plastic cord, string, buttonhole thread or bulldog clips.

Tie-dyeing can be done using hand or machine dye, following the manufacturer's instructions. To achieve an even colour the fabric needs to move freely, so make sure your dye bath is big enough. Dampen the fabric before placing it in the dye to prevent it floating and to help achieve an even colour.

1 To make lines, pleat the fabric accordion fashion and bind at regular intervals.

2 Tie in circular items such as coins, lentils, marbles or even saucers to make circles of different sizes.

3 To create a lacy speckled effect, roll the fabric round a piece of string. Pull the string ends round to form a loop and slide the fabric up to make a small gathered circle. Tie the string securely.

4 To make a circular cobweb pattern start tying as if you were making a circle as in step 2, but spread the ties out down the cloth.

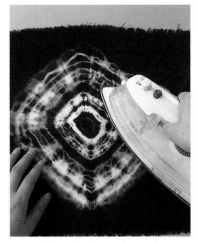

5 When the fabric has achieved the desired colour remove it from the dye and rinse in cold water until it runs clear. Remove the bindings and wash the fabric to remove any excess dye. Iron while still damp.

TEMPLATES

Enlarge the templates on a photocopier, or trace the design and draw a grid of evenly spaced squares over your tracing. Draw a larger grid on to another piece of paper and copy the outline square by square. Draw over the lines to make sure they are continuous.

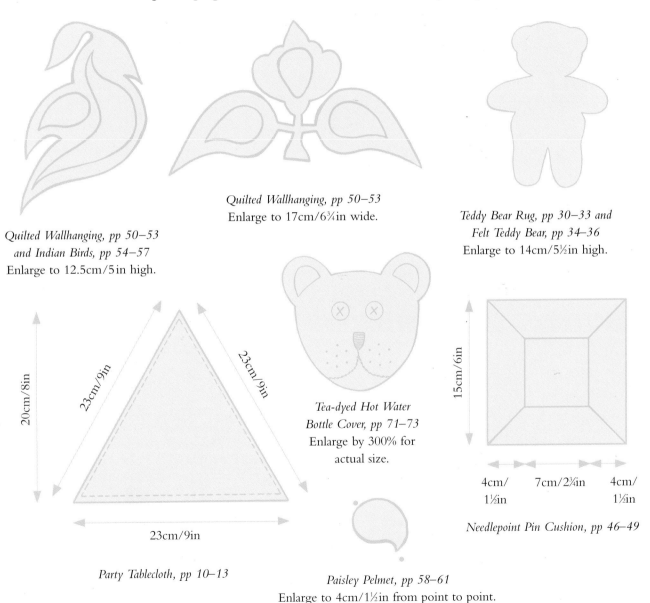

Quilted Wallhanging, pp 50–53
Enlarge to 17cm/6¾in wide.

Quilted Wallhanging, pp 50–53
and Indian Birds, pp 54–57
Enlarge to 12.5cm/5in high.

Teddy Bear Rug, pp 30–33 and
Felt Teddy Bear, pp 34–36
Enlarge to 14cm/5½in high.

Tea-dyed Hot Water
Bottle Cover, pp 71–73
Enlarge by 300% for
actual size.

20cm/8in

23cm/9in

23cm/9in

23cm/9in

Party Tablecloth, pp 10–13

Paisley Pelmet, pp 58–61
Enlarge to 4cm/1½in from point to point.

15cm/6in

4cm/
1½in

7cm/2¾in

4cm/
1½in

Needlepoint Pin Cushion, pp 46–49

Lilac Devoré Blind, pp 77–79 Enlarge by 300% for actual size.

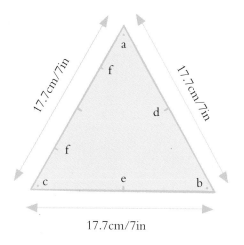

Lavender Bags, pp 19–21

ACKNOWLEDGEMENTS

Thanks to the following project makers:
Penny Boylan for making the Tea-dyed Hot Water Bottle Cover p.71, Velvet-edged Throw p.8, Dyed Gift Wrap and Tags p.41, and Dip-dyed Album Cover p.63; **Judith Gussin** for making the Party Tablecloth p.10, Rainbow Cosmetic Bag, p.17, Lavender Bags p.19, Block-printed Cushion p.26, Teddy Bear Rug p.30, Felt Teddy Bears p.35, Quilted Wallhanging p.50, Indian Birds p.54, Paisley Pelmet p.58, Patchwork Toy Bag p.69, and Silk Cushion p.75; **Sheila Gussin** for designing the Teddy Bear Rug p.30, Felt Teddy Bears p.35, and making the Needlepoint Pin Cushion p.46, and the Beaded Curtain p.14; **Susie Stokoe** for the Tie-dye Duvet Cover p.22, Batik Napkin p.37, Dip-dyed Lampshade p.43, Silk Tablerunner p. 65, and the Lilac Devoré Blind p.77.

SUPPLIERS

The materials and equipment needed for dyeing fabric are quite readily available. Large department stores sell a range of fabrics and some dyes and fabric paint. Specialist dyes, fabrics already prepared for dyeing and printing, and space-dyed fabrics and embroidery threads can be purchased through mail order.

UK

21st Century Yarns
Unit 14
Earl Soham Lodge
Earl Soham
Suffolk IP13 7SA
Tel: (01394) 387659
Acid dyes, cold-water reactive dyes, undyed silk and wool embroidery yarns, space-dyed fabric and embroidery threads

Whaleys (Bradford) Ltd
Harris Court
Great Horton Road
Bradford
West Yorkshire BD7 4EQ
Tel: (01274) 576718
Fabrics prepared for printing and dyeing

George Weil & Sons Ltd
1 Old Portsmouth Road
Peasmarsh
Guildford
Surrey GU3 1LZ
Tel: (01483) 565800
Printing inks, fabric paints

John Lewis
Oxford Street
London W1A 1EX
and branches
Tel: (020) 7629 7711
Fabrics, fabric paints, interfacing, bonding web and haberdashery

Supermend
P.O. Box 300
Basildon
Essex SS14 3RT
Tel: (01268) 271244
Bonding powder

Creative Beadcraft
Denmark Works
Sheepcote Dell Road
Beamond End
Nr Amersham
Buckinghamshire HP7 0RZ
Tel: (01494) 715606
Beads

Silken Strands
20 Y Rhos
Bangor LL57 2LT
Tel: (01248) 362361
Shisha glass, machine embroidery threads (floss)

Barnyarns Ltd
Freepost
NEA8008
Thirsk YO7 3ZZ
Tel: (0800 018 3791)
Machine embroidery threads

USA

Dharmsa Trading Co.
PO Box 150916
San Rafael, CA 94915
Tel: (800) 542 5227
www.dharmatrading.com

Nasco Arts and Crafts
901 Janesville Avenue
Fort Wilkinson, WI 53538
Tel (800) 558 9595
www.nascofa.com

Dick Blick Art Materials
PO Box 1267
695 US Highway 150 East
Galesburg, IL 61402
www.dickblick.com

Art Supply Warehouse
5325 Departure Drive
North Raleigh, NC 27616
Tel: (919) 878-5077
www.aswexpress.com

OPAS, Inc (Olympic Potter's and Artist's Supply)
1822 Harrison Avenue, NW
Olympia, WA 98502
Tel: (360) 943-5332
www.olywa.net/opas/index.html

INDEX